MW01596434

100 SIMPLE WAYS TO
CONNECT
WITH
GOD

Any Time, Anywhere,
Every Day!

Dr. Veronica B. Winston

100 Simple Ways To Connect With God
All Scripture references are taken from the *King James Version* of the Bible.

ISBN: 978-1-63541-008-2
Copyright November 2017
Published by Bill Winston Ministries
P.O. Box 947
Oak Park, IL 60303-0947

Copies of 100 Simple Ways To Connect With God
can be obtained through:
Royal Christian Bookstores & Cafés
7600 W. Roosevelt Road
Forest Park, IL 60130
(708) 697-5333
www.royalchristianbookstores.com
www.billwinston.org

DEDICATION

This book is dedicated to those who "keep it real," knowing that in spite of their imperfections, character flaws, missteps, and carnal moments, God still desires a relationship with them, and they unashamedly come boldly before Him, with the full expectation that He will complete His work in them.

To the people whose lives have been radically changed because one day they permanently connected with the God who is really, really good to know and hang out with.

And to those who refuse to let go of their God, who remain steadfast in their faith despite adverse circumstances, having discovered that it's indeed true that without Him we can do nothing. And to you, to nudge you to get Him involved in everything on your journey of faith and to live an exciting life!

TABLE OF CONTENTS

INTRODUCTION

Connecting with God is all about *relationship*. Getting to know the God who loves you, saved you, and planned a good life for you. It's where you learn what moves His heart, and where you allow Him to move yours.

Connection takes place when we respond to our loving God drawing us into eternal life in Him, in whom we live and move and have our being (Acts 17:28). This union is so strong that the apostle John describes Jesus' sacrifice on the cross as "that we might live through him (1 John 4:9).

"Eternal life" describes the life and ministry of Jesus, which *every* believer now has (1 John 1:2, 5:11). We are called to be like Jesus (1 John 3:2) to walk as he walked (1 John 2:6) and to protect the eternal life which abides in us by loving our brother (1 John 3:14-15).

The goal is not to connect and disconnect, but to *dwell in* or *live in God* always, by dwelling in love (1 John 4:16) and walking in truth (3 John 3-4). God's greatest commandments to love God and love our neighbor set a compass in our hearts, pointing back to God, so every deed and encounter can be assessed if it is truly on the path of life.

Pursuing God with relentless passion keeps our love for Him alive and infuses us with His love and grace to enrich our other relationships. Engaging God's Word (the Bible) and His Holy Spirit continually are as vital to our soul's health as oxygen and blood are to our bodies. We regulate the pump of our soul's "heart" by communicating and communing with God. If we neglect the feeding and nourishing of our relationship with God, the soul's heart stops pumping, and our soul grows cold and rigid towards God; dull, unfeeling, dispassionate, distant lukewarm, and unresponsive.

We endanger our very lives into becoming dead to God and alive to sin, instead of alive to God and dead to sin (Romans 6:11). Jesus prayed for our union with Him and the Father (John 17:21-23) that we would be one. As good friends and family, the more we "hang out," the more like Him we sound and act. This is the destiny of every believer. (Romans 8:29)

God loves us soooo much that He will freely give us all things we ask of Him (Romans 8:32, Psalm 84:11, Matthew 7:7-8). Answered prayer begins with our commitment to and the pursuit of a living, active and, at times, exciting union or connection with God. God searches our hearts and seeks to develop a purity in our motives and attitudes. That is why the journey to answered prayer (connection time) is as important as the destination.

God is drawing us to converse with our Creator on a daily basis. Receiving salvation is our accepting God's invitation to journey with Him throughout the rest of our lives, and follow Him as He leads us down the best possible path to a fulfilling life now and for eternity.

Spending time with God is not complicated, mysterious or mystical. It is as normal as having a conversation with the person sitting next to you. It does not have to be emotional, but it can be. It does not have to be long, but it is engaging when it is.

Time spent with God is when we get to know Him. Some call it a "devotional" time in the morning. I call it "connect" time at any time of the day or night. It is where we express our love and devotion towards Him. In turn, He speaks to us, through Bible verses, revelation of a hidden truth just revealed, or through an inward witness or knowing. He can speak audibly, but usually hearing from God is an assurance within our heart.

Connection with God keeps His presence a continuous living reality.

We "connect" through many methods of interacting with Him and His Word, the Bible. Even though we cannot visibly see Him, the more we acknowledge Him, the more real He becomes to us.

Let's review some definitions of the word *connect* to give us clarity:

1. to link two things 2. associate somebody or something with another 3. get along well 4. establish telecommunication link for somebody (Microsoft® Encarta® Dictionary).

1. to hook up, link up, unite, bond, associate, relate, get along, hit it off (Thesaurus.com. *Roget's 21st Century Thesaurus, Third Edition*. Philip Lief Group 2009. http://www.thesaurus.com/browse/connect (accessed: October 27, 2017).

1. to become joined 2. to have or establish rapport ("Connect." Merriam-Webster.com. Accessed October 27, 2017. https://www.merriam-webster.com/dictionary/connect).

1. to come together to form a single unit; unite, fuse, marry, unify ("Connect." Merriam-Webster.com. Accessed October 27, 2017. https://www.merriam-webster.com/thesaurus/connect).

Did some keywords stand out to you? *To link two things…to unite… to join…establish rapport…marry… unify…to get along well.* That is exactly what God wants with us! A divine hook-up, a BFF for life and even beyond! But more than that, an all-knowing, all-seeing God invites us to walk with Him daily as He reveals His true nature through His Word, during our prayer time, and through life experiences with others. Adam, Enoch, and Noah walked with God. Abraham was a friend of God. The Lord was with Joseph, Moses, Joshua and David. And He is with YOU!

Developing the **habit** of daily talking with and listening to God is as important as the act itself. Habits can make or break us. Good habits consistently followed produce good things in our lives, so committing to meeting with God every day to "check in" with Him before the day gets too hectic will prepare us for making better choices during the day.

God calls us, His Church, a "House of Prayer." Prayer is a part of a wider range of activities spent with God where our union with Him and conscious connection with Him is strengthened. In the pages that follow are descriptions of what we can do during those times. Be encouraged to try several of them, as the Holy Spirit leads you. (Isaiah 56:7, Mark 11:17)

To most of the people around you, it may not make sense to begin your day talking to a God who you cannot see. It may seem absurd to expect this same God to give you clear direction on matters that you must tend to that day. It may seem ludicrous to expect that by reading a Bible written hundreds and thousands of years ago, you can learn principles to live by in the 21st century. Well, ignore the naysayers! God has a lot to reveal to us, and we do not want to miss a word of it!

By spending time daily in the presence of our Creator, we can get to know Him and understand His plan for our lives. When we connect with the Eternal, our perspective changes from what is only possible with men, to what is possible with God. Many of life's challenges can be resolved and overcome with God's guidance.

There is no guaranteed formula for what will achieve your "divine connection" on any given day. But the truths that anchor our souls and feed our spirits come from time spent with God. Hearing God's will through His Word helps us to develop a genuine personal relationship with God. When the storm winds blow, our daily time with God will have established a spiritual relationship that no naturally-based disaster or spiritual attack can destroy. (Matthew 7:24-27)

Keeping our connection with God strong and solid is crucial to holding steady as the world declines into more ungodliness. Jesus (the Word) is the truth we stand on, and the Holy

Spirit empowers us to keep standing and ultimately prevail. Our fortitude, endurance and perseverance through hard times is a powerful witness to help others press through the darkness in pursuit of the light, showing them that the power of God is a reality in our lives.

Just like our conversion, our time with God is personal and intimate, and only our own. When there is no one else to encourage us and keep us from giving up on life, God is there. Jesus tells us to always pray and not faint. (Luke 18:1)

100 Simple Ways to Connect with God gives you a variety of ways to open up your heart to God to receive the reality of His love and the assurance of His guidance. There is no set rule on how long to take or how many different methods to apply in a single devotional time. What works beautifully one day may seem dry and unengaging the next day! What brings breakthrough one week may seem like toil the next week. The power is not in a formula to duplicate, but in the faith that comes alive when the

Holy Spirit reveals the living Christ in you.

Spending time with God regularly will train your spirit to connect in a way that is most meaningful to you at that particular place and time. We should leave our private time with God refreshed and renewed. It takes time together to really know a person you intend to marry. Getting to know God is no different, and we are with Him for eternity. (Hebrews 8:10-12)

Ultimately, you will want to discover your own "flow" with God.

The time your neighbor spends with God may not be enough for you, given your calling and responsibilities. Avoid the temptation of comparing your "connection" times with others. Just enjoy it!

Can I give you a word of recommendation? Please allow yourself enough time to get past the impatience of the flesh. Quality time takes just that—quality time. Prayer and praise are fine on the fly, in the shower, in the car, on the train. But on a regular basis throughout the week, take a little more time to slow down and get centered. God is already seeking you when you decide to respond to His drawing.

Relationship-building activities like worshipping and praising God, meditating His Word, and journaling will probably not produce fireworks and standing ovations. What it will bring is an inner peace and a satisfaction for having put God first in your day and letting Him put every other thing into proper perspective.

Daily connecting with God brings an unseen stability that makes you ok in spite of what may come your way. It may bring ideas that challenge you to get out of your comfort zone and get moving! Or it might convict you of being way too busy, where you allowed your natural obligations to outpace your spiritual ability to manage them.

God may want to highlight areas for your personal improvement, or He may want to inspire you to think out of the box and let Him do more through you! No two days are ever the same. If you are bored with your devotional times, God probably is too! Do something different! Try a variety of connecting ideas in this book.

Before long you will find yourself talking to God spontaneously (He *is* living inside your spirit!) You will be aware of His presence at crossroad-level decisions. You will question yourself "does this action or response reflect the Christ within me?" before you go off on someone. Your heart will choose to show kindness to others instead of putting selfish interests first.

Big visions and dreams come from a big God! He rejoices to bring His own into good success! When opportunity knocks, only preparation can open the door. Time with God is the best preparation for a great future!

Last, the God who loves us so greatly looks forward to an eternity of relationship and connection with us. His Son Jesus sacrificed His life so we could reconnect to Him, and to the quality of life that died when Adam's sin in the garden of Eden unplugged us from our Source of Life. As we daily connect, the rivers of living water can once again refresh our weary souls and renew our faith to live with passion and purpose, with Jesus and the Holy

Spirit directing our lives, and giving us a reason to live.

Daily communing with God is, I believe, the best training ground for building good friendships and marriages. Without God's life flowing through us, we communicate from a depleted and bankrupt soul. Instead of adding value and building others up, our words tear down and wound, most times unintentionally.

The end goal of connecting with God extends beyond our own personal benefit. It is the starting point to healing our own wounds and positions us to finish God's end-time work in the earth through His heart of compassion as a living sacrifice.

As we humble ourselves and get real with God about who we are and why we are here, He will do a major "upgrade" in our lives. He will erase our soul's hard drive crippled by the eternal hacker and enemy of our souls, and download a new and enhanced, divinely designed version, equipped with all the spyware and firewall protection we need to successfully advance the kingdom of God!

A WORD TO BEGINNERS

There is no need to overwhelm yourself and try to do every step referenced in this book the first week! Take your time, and try things at a slower pace. For example, choose one method from each section of **Speaking, Reading, Listening** and **Writing**, as time permits. Speak a written prayer, read a chapter in your Bible, listen to a worship song, and write notes in a journal. Voila! You just connected with God! And don't forget to listen.

100 Simple Ways to Connect with God

"Then shall ye call upon me, and ye shall go and pray unto me, and I will hearken unto you. And ye shall seek me, and find *me*, when ye shall search for me with all your heart."

Jeremiah 29:12-13

SPEAKING

1

Praying by Reading Prayer Confessions is a simple and effective way to pray to God. Here we learn to pray according to God's will and perspective, not complaining or whining, but believing that what He said shall come to pass. Prayer should be sprinkled generously with thanksgiving and praise. Using biblically-based confessions assures that He hears us and that we shall have our petitions answered. (1 John 5:14-15)

2 **Praying with Thanksgiving** is thanking God for anything and everything that comes to mind that you are thankful to Him for. It's showing appreciation and gratefulness for how good He is to us. Even in adversity, we thank God that He sees all, and has worked it out for our good. We acknowledge that we owe all we have and all we are to Him, and we will not forget it! (Psalm 107:21-22, Ephesians 5:20)

3 **Praying with Praise**, recognize His awesome qualities and works, listing them and expanding upon them as you praise Him, with hands lifted or even offering a dance of praise before Him. God's vision is to bring us from a place of desolation and mourning to becoming people of glory and praise, thereby drawing the whole world to Him. (Psalm 146:2, 71:8, 119:164, Isaiah 62:1-7, Hebrews 13:15)

4 **Worshipping God** in the spirit and in truth, adoring His greatness and character. We know Him because His Word has revealed His nature, and the Bible is full of accounts where He has manifested His goodness to many. Musicians will use their instruments in worship, dancers will dance, artists will create, poets will compose…use your gift to honor God today. (Psalm 95:6-7, 150, John 4:23-24)

5 **Singing to God** from our hearts or along with a praise and worship recording will create an atmosphere of heaven, as we lift our voices to God. It can refresh our hearts, refocus our minds on the important, and pull us out of our fleshly thoughts. Singing anointed praise songs to God heals broken hearts, refreshes our souls, excites (or calms) our spirits, encourages us and fills us with God's presence. (Psalm 149:1-4, Ephesians 5:18-19)

6 **Praying Using Prayer Lists** will help us to focus on specific people, things and events that we desire God's blessing and intervention on. Loved ones, schools, city, state and federal government officials by name, your church activity calendar, your meetings, projects, goals and dreams, daily tasks, current issues… the prayer list possibility is endless! Let God lead you on what needs prayer cover that day. As the list grows, designate items for each day of the week. (Philippians 1:3-4)

7 Praying Over Prayer Requests that others have submitted to you or to a local church or ministry will connect your heart with the needs of others. It is always good to go beyond our own needs and requests to God and include our loved ones, our church family, and neighbors. Do not forget that addictions, abuse, violence, hatred and anger are also unspoken cries for help. (2 Thessalonians 3:1, Mark 5:1-20)

8 **Praying in Tongues**, an ability that follows being baptized with the Holy Spirit, enables us to pray according to God's perfect will, even when we are not mentally aware of the details of the need or of the solution. This may take a few minutes or a few hours, as God leads you. Your spirit will truly rejoice as you pray in this "heavenly language." (Mark 16:17, Acts 19:1-6, 1 Corinthians 2:6-14, 14:2, Romans 8:26-28)

9 **Praying Conversational Prayer** is perhaps the simplest and most common way of praying that people are familiar with. It is just talking to God, asking Him to move in the earth on behalf of others or for yourself. This is one way we can be "praying always" (Ephesians 6:18, Colossians 1:3). Hebrews 11:6 says God is a rewarder of those who diligently seek Him. Our time of prayer (which is never in vain), can transform an unfulfilled life to one of power and glory to impact nations! (Matthew 6:6, Isaiah 55)

10

Praying in Agreement with Another is a way you two can agree as touching a particular need, that God's will shall be done. Others can help us see our need from another perspective, contribute godly wisdom, and boost our faith, as they believe with us. Jesus promises to be present with us as we pray with another. (Matthew 18:19)

11

Praying from a Structured Format allows you to manage your time better by mapping out the different activities planned for that day's devotion. Allotting each connection activity a specified time period helps when time is limited and you don't want to overlook items God placed on your heart. Remember, the power is not in the formula we follow, but in the connection that takes place through a wide variety of ways we seek His face. (Daniel 6:10)

12

Praying in Intercession is where we pray to God for others. We empathize with their need and ask God on their behalf to provide whatever is needed. We base our requests on God's will as revealed in His Word, the Bible. God may place a strong feeling of compassion upon you, and grace to pray for them until God's answer is assured. Catch the vision—for nations are already interceding together! (1 Samuel 12:23, Zechariah 8:20-23, 1 Timothy 2:1)

13 Praying with Travail

happens when the Holy Spirit engulfs you with such an all-encompassing desire for breakthrough or deliverance of individuals, people groups, troubling current events or impending disaster that you cry, wail, and perhaps groan, as if you were giving birth to a child. This type of prayer is usually only as the Spirit of God comes upon you with this urgency. It is uncool to fake it, so please don't. (Romans 8:26, Galatians 4:19)

14

Communing with God is a heartfelt intimate conversation (spoken or silent) with God, where His peaceful presence is distinctly felt in your innermost being. You are peacefully focused on Him and on what He is revealing to you. Please, let the inner "energizer bunny" slow down periodically, to refresh and regroup. Our daily connecting with God serves to recalibrate our inner man (from life's potholes) to realign with heaven's purposes and plans. (Isaiah 26:9, Psalm 4:4)

15

Prophesying the Word over the areas you are praying for is a bold declaration of God's will being done regardless of how it looks presently. Revelation 19:10 says, "for the testimony of Jesus is the spirit of prophecy." When we declare what God has accomplished in Christ Jesus for us on the cross, we speak that reality into our own lives and those we intercede for. (Romans 4:17, 2 Kings 7)

16

Prayer Walking is effective alone or in groups around your neighborhood. As you pass every home, school, business and gathering place, reflect on those who visit, work, and live there. Put yourselves in their shoes, feel their needs as you pray. Take spiritual ownership of your community, to keep them covered with prayers of safety, prosperity and salvation. (Genesis 3:8, Joshua 1:1-9)

READING

17 **Reading through the Bible is** an excellent way to learn about God, His plan for mankind, and to build your new identity in Christ. Reading from Genesis to Revelation will provide the "knowledge building blocks" that form the basis of your faith, strength, wisdom, direction and relationship with God. Identify a hunger or curiosity to answer, and let God surprise you by answering as your read! (Luke 4:16, Exodus 24:7, Nehemiah 8)

18

Studying the Bible is the next step up from reading, where we discover truths of God's kingdom that are below the surface. Studying starts the river of revelation to flow, as God Himself teaches us through the Holy Spirit. We discover truths that we may apply to our lives to bring about change for the better. Using print and digital aids to research a wealth of topics will enhance your learning experience. (2 Timothy 2:15)

19

Meditation of Bible Verses is yet another step where we slow down further to let the "roots" of a particular verse or teaching grow deep in our hearts. When these truths are rooted in us, and we keep our hearts sensitive to God, nothing can steal the reality of these truths from us. We believe them, we know them, we see them (even though they are unseen in the natural), we live by them, and they produce God's promises in our lives. (Joshua 1:8, Psalm 1:1-3, Psalm 119:15)

20

Memorizing Scripture used to be commonplace in the Church. It renews our minds and our thinking, filling us with God's wisdom for daily living. When God's Word is in our hearts, He will speak to us through those very words when we need it. Record key verses on a card file or digital note file on your smart device. They can be used to support a goal, address a personal weakness, fulfill a vision or resist an attack. The Word works! (Psalm 119:11, Proverbs 2)

21

Sowing the Word is taking a specific Bible verse, memorizing it, meditating it, getting it deep in our hearts and flooding our minds, until it becomes so real that it begins to manifest in our lives. The sower sows the Word, and the entire kingdom of God is based on this principle. As you sleep, that seed is growing into a harvest, even if you do not know how! It's God's miracle of increase. We sow with the expectation of producing that harvest. (Mark 4:14-32, Luke 8:11)

22

Reading Inspirational Books and devotionals written by believers in Christ can impart to us decades of learning and experience from believers who walk with God! We are mentored, corrected, motivated and jump-started by their insight into wisdom received from God, and the results as they walked a life of faith. Connecting with them connects us to God. A book is the next best thing to a live or video teaching. Authors become your personal spiritual coach! (John 21:25, Revelation 1:11, 3 John 2)

23

Reading Secular Inspirational Books for our personal or professional development inspire us to be our best, and teach us how to navigate this life's journey in the midst of an ever-changing culture. These resources help us prepare ourselves to serve God and others as best we can. God adds His "super" to our "natural" knowledge and gives us insight that promotes us. Natural skill prepared the disciples to become "fishers of men" therefore become proficient learners in both realms! (Exodus 18:13-26, Matthew 4:19, Psalm 75:6)

24

Reviewing Sermon, Bible Class and Conference Notes reinforce the tremendous revelation received at these meetings. God sent the speakers to perfect you for the work of the ministry, so He must desire to manifest at least a portion of what was taught to you! Ponder how to apply what you have learned. Put it on your calendar for a plan of action. When you walk out that truth, you complete the cycle of faith by being doers of the Word and not hearers only. (Matthew 7:24-27, Ephesians 4:11-13, James 1:22-27, 3 John 3, 4)

25

Reviewing Staff Meeting Notes will keep ministry employees in tune with the leader and reinforce what they have highlighted to you in their teachings. Implement specific principles they have taught in your department. Church leadership is operating on a God-given vision, and their staff must see what they see to execute the vision accurately. These teachings reflect the heart of your leader, and of God. (Deuteronomy 1:1-3, John 13)

26

Attending Bible School may be your solution when casual study doesn't satisfy your craving for knowledge to equip you for your calling to serve God. Learning from a variety of seasoned believers gives perspective to your faith. Seminaries focus more on what historical theologians have written about the Bible, so make sure to research your school choice to ensure it can meet your expectations. (Acts 19:9-10)

27 **Reviewing Personal Journal Notes** will remind you of what God has been revealing during your private times with Him. Each nugget of truth has eternal value, so review them periodically to establish God's truths as an integral part of your daily lifestyle. See which entries would be beneficial to share with others to enhance their spiritual growth. Look for patterns where God is trying to get a message to you. (2 Timothy 4:13)

28

Reviewing the Prophecies spoken to you personally or given during a church service keep you seeing things from heaven's perspective. Usually, prophecies project the bigness of our God, His plans for our future, warnings, and the all-encompassing dominion He exerts in the earth through His chosen. Prophecies should be prayed through, as we seek God for their fulfillment. (1 Timothy 1:18, 4:14)

REFLECTING

29

Reflection and Quiet Time is the term used for getting still before God and focusing our minds on Him or whatever matter we are bringing to Him. We stop the racing of our own thoughts and let His thoughts rise up from our spirits, from the inside of us. Purposely see life in the future according to what God has promised in His Word, and not according to natural circumstances. Enjoy God in the stillness of the moment, being aware that He is real and present with you. (Psalm 46:10)

30 Reflection by Invitation.

Don't be surprised if God picks a time and place for devotion Himself! He may softly awaken you at a quiet time in the middle of the night, or He may speak to you in a certain place you did not expect. Oh, what an honor and privilege to be summoned into God's "secret place" to convene at His request! It may be to pray, to receive teaching or just to talk as good friends. (Psalm 65:4, 1 Samuel 3:4)

31

Reflection for Repentance and Refreshing is beneficial when we have missed God and chosen the way of the flesh. When love, joy, peace, faith, kindness and self-control have given way to impatience, criticism and negativity, it is time to pull back and regroup! Confessing our sins, repenting before God, and receiving His forgiveness and cleansing will empower us to continue in our walk of faith free from guilt and condemnation from the enemy. (1 John 1:9)

32

Reflection and Watching in Prayer take place when we see areas of concern and take them to God in prayer. Natural hindrances and mishaps may reflect symptoms of deeper trouble on the horizon. Nip it in the bud and pray for God to intervene before the enemy's large-scale deception and destruction can proceed. Be sober and vigilant (1 Peter 5:8). The sooner we detect danger and pray against it, the harder it is for the enemy to succeed in his efforts to sabotage us. (Matthew 26:41)

33

Reflection and Hearing from God usually happen when we get still and allow His thoughts to fill our thoughts. Create an environment conducive and welcoming to His voice. Sometimes the Holy Spirit may even interrupt as we carry on daily activities, to deliver a message of revelation that inspires us or answers a previous prayer prayed. Expect to be taught by God! He promises that all shall know Him, from the least to the greatest! (Hebrews 8:10-11, Psalm 32:8)

34

Reflection and Interpretation of Tongues. We are instructed in scripture to pray that we may interpret when we pray in tongues. This is useful especially when we are praying in tongues for a specific reason, for clarity, confirmation or guidance. When life becomes overwhelming, talking it over with God in tongues can release what is in your heart to God's heart. His solutions can be worked out as we pray through, and inner peace will result. (1 Corinthians 14:13)

35

Reflection on the Scriptures. Has curiosity over a scripture verse ever inspired an in-depth study of the Word? Taking time to reflect on scriptures we read can open up revelation far beyond our natural thinking and understanding. It may reveal new avenues on how to apply Bible truth to a situation you are facing or stimulate faith that empowers you to go beyond perceived limitations. Faith arises as the Word builds us up, bringing God's promises within our reach. (Acts 20:32)

36

Reflection and Personal Evaluation. Periodically it is a good idea to take an assessment of where you stand with God, with others, and with fulfilling your roles and responsibilities. Are you giving it your best? Are you serving others and reflecting God's character? Are you diligently pursuing Him and watchful to cut off areas where the enemy may be trying to gain entry into your life? Cut out the fluff and get back to kingdom business! (2 Corinthians 13:5)

37

Reflection and Waiting is taking time to pause and listen to our hearts. Do not rush into your own agenda. Wait to see where God leads in today's devotional time. Guidance will come as a desire to study a scripture, read a book, write in a journal, and pray from a list or from another area where curiosity and hunger direct us. Relish the freedom to be present with Him, free from external pressures. Let us be like Mary and choose that good part by taking time to hear from God. (Luke 10:42, Psalm 27:14, 37:34)

LISTENING

38

Listening to Sermons and Teachings from services, websites, TV, CDs, DVDs, MP3s, and wave files are all good ways to keep the Word before our eyes and our ears, inspiring us as we go about our day. We prosper our souls, renew our minds and set our affection on heavenly things. Hearing the Word is better than the carnal inner chatter of an unfocused mind. This would be an additional activity after your private fellowship with the Lord. (Proverbs 8:6-21)

39

Watching Inspirational Movies is a good way to reinforce Biblical truths in the context of stories of everyday life. It complements a positive and wholesome home atmosphere for children when godly values are reinforced in an entertaining way. Our hearts are lifted and refreshed when goodness is treasured and celebrated. Let us be watchful of who we allow to sow seeds and images into our imaginations. Take a welcome departure from the culture of explicitly sexual and violence-based entertainment.

40

Listening to a CD Bible or an Audio Bible is a good background listening alternative to secular radio or television. You can access so much more truth from passages previously overlooked. It is also a good way to supplement personal time spent reading the Word. You may find that discovering verses drawn to your attention by hearing is a pleasant change from reading. It exposes us to a broader range of Bible chapters in one sitting than we may usually read in an average day. (Psalm 119:97)

41

Listening to God speak from a variety of avenues can be fun! He may speak through an inward witness, through the scriptures, a song, a friend, a TV broadcast, a preacher, a book, or even a beautiful landscape or sunset. He gives confirmations, new insights or even warnings through uneasiness or a check in our spirit. Be open to receive and appreciate it when it comes. Anticipate and expect His "divine instant messaging" throughout your day! (John 10:27)

42

Listening to Praise and Worship Music keeps our hearts and our environment charged with excitement, gratefulness and faith. The anointing seems to wash away the elements that clog our connection with God and leaves us refreshed and ready for the next new challenge. We can listen while we drive, work, exercise, take a bubble bath or do housework. Music can bypass the mind and minister directly to our hearts. (Ephesians 5:19)

43

Listening to Soaking Music is when you choose soothing music specifically composed for "soaking" in God's presence. There is no agenda, no talking, just being with Him. Here we are totally focused on God, not doing anything else, resting our bodies and minds from endless activity to be at peace and one with God. We are always listening for instructions from our Father God, through the Holy Spirit, as we engage in all of these connection methods!

SANCTIFYING

44

Denying the Flesh is sometimes required to set aside longer periods of time to hear from God and separate from the busyness of life. We can fast food, or unnecessary activities, unedifying conversation, media and digital communication, excess socializing and leisurely pleasures. These easily crowd out or replace our connection time with God. Feeding our hungry spirit and fasting our fleshly desires is a good habit that brings beneficial results. (Galatians 5:16-17)

45

Fasting and Prayer is a powerful combination when a situation demands more spiritual sensitivity or strength to obtain answers and results. When the flesh is denied, our spirit benefits from the whole of our attention engaged with God. Jesus taught that fasting and prayer empower us over spiritual opposition. (Mark 9:29, Acts 13:3, Nehemiah 1:4, Isaiah 58)

46

Fasting at Work is sometimes necessary, especially when hindering forces have blocked forward movement on projects that you know God has assigned to you. It allows heightened focus to produce results and sometimes is practiced quite unintentionally! You can sense a "window of opportunity" while working, to stay with a project until completion, as if God Himself is holding back hindering forces on your behalf.

47 **Taking Communion** in your private time is an act of faith in the resurrection power and blood of Jesus as you apply it while receiving the bread and juice. We remember that when Jesus died, we died; he arose, and we arose; He went to heaven, and we too are seated in heavenly places in Christ. His sacrifice purchased our freedom from sin and restored God's blessings to mankind, for those who choose to follow and serve Him. (1 Corinthians 11:23-31, Ephesians 1:19-23)

WRITING

48

Writing in a Journal is a valuable practice to preserve the revelation received during your times with God. The treasures of wisdom, answers to questions, and insights received over the years is your written record of time well spent seeking and hearing from God. After a time of praying in tongues, get ready to write, for God is surely speaking! Take notes as you read the Bible. Prepare teachings to share, write prayer requests and answers. (Revelation 1:11)

49

Writing Prayers is an excellent way to preserve your requests to God and maintain your focus, as you keep matters before Him and hold fast the profession of your faith. It keeps the answer you believe Him for before you and builds faith every time you hear yourself thanking God that it is already done, based on the Word of God. You will find your thoughts and expectations begin to align with your words. Finally, record each date as it comes to pass.

50

Writing Plans, Tasks and Priority Management is not traditionally considered an important part of devotion, but as we acknowledge God in planning our daily tasks, He promises to direct our path. Knowing your weekly schedule early on will help you stay focused on the important matters and minimize wasting time. Be open to pruning the unnecessary. Keep your goals before you. We must be about our Father's business as kingdom citizens! (Matthew 6:33, Proverbs 3:5-6, 4:26-27)

51

Writing for Projects, Sermons, and Teachings. Ideas seem to flow freely during devotion times, so why not seize the moment of an open heaven and let God give you the insight to tackle those challenging projects before you! He is the Source of all true wisdom and has reserved it for His own children. God brings such clarity and creative ideas during our time with Him, so be ready with pen and paper or device when the God-inspired download begins! (Proverbs 2:1-8)

52

Writing a Gratitude Journal. While on a recent vacation I was so grateful for the trip that I felt compelled to list all the good things God had been doing for me to ensure I really enjoyed my rest and relaxation. Keeping a grateful journal keeps us mentally disciplined to think thoughts that build up and lead to more good things. Gratefulness is easy in the good times, but a sacrificial weapon to resist a negative mindset in times of adversity. (1 Thessalonians 5:18)

53

Writing Out Your Frustrations and Complaints. This is not really a practice I recommend to do frequently, but every once in a while we need to let off steam, and it's better we write it in a journal than explode on whoever has the misfortune to be near us! Put it on paper and get it out of your thoughts! Then cast every one of those cares upon God, trust Him, then act in faith as if every issue has been resolved by God on your behalf. (Psalm 55:22)

54 Writing Out Your Own Chastisement.

When you know you could and should do better, giving yourself a word of correction might be just the thing to snap you out of complacency and compromise and into discipline and purpose. Own your behavior. Making excuses only causes us to lower our standards and our expectations of ourselves. Effective correction inspires repentance and righteous behavior. "Straighten up and fly right!" (Hebrews 12:6-13)

ORGANIZING

55

Organizing Your Study Environment periodically helps to keep mental clarity and order as your prayer materials, journal notes, reference materials and media products begin to increase. These materials aid us in Bible study and keeping multiple areas before God and in our prayers. Do not let them get overwhelming! An attractive and orderly environment inspires inner fruitfulness. Even God uses purging as a process to get us to bear more fruit! (John 15:2)

56

Organizing Notes, Books and Journals are, in my opinion, as important as all the other areas listed in this book. Inevitably, papers will pile up, and your devotional hideaway can become a disaster zone! Our God has a lot to share, and we ought to be organized to keep up with Him! You probably have enough notes for a year of sermons, so index your journals by topic and add tabs for easy reference. Keeping things tidy and accessible will keep your journals inspiring and inviting.

57

Organize Your Life. The apostle Paul admonished Titus (Titus 1:5) to "set in order the things that are wanting…" when unruliness tried to invade the church. What needs to be set in order in your life? Are you following the basics of the faith? Water baptism, Holy Spirit baptism, walking by faith and in love, praying, attending and volunteering at church, paying tithes, giving offerings, sharing your faith and attending your church's new members' classes are foundational to your life of faith. Start here and reclaim the excitement of being born again!

58

Organizing Project Materials. Invariably, during devotion, God may also give you ideas on the various projects you are currently working on, or for meetings in the future. Having a notebook with sections for each current and future project makes it easy at the time of inspiration to jot things down in the right place for easy access. The same goes for your yearly calendar of important meetings and events. You can record ideas months in advance and not miss the unexpected nuggets given to you during your prayer time.

59

Typing Notes and Forms for frequently used prayers and study materials will make time with God more pleasurable because you are not squinting to read your "chicken scratch" notes! Using forms to record what is important keeps you accountable to yourself to follow through. Better yet, record your work log on a digital device, and you will always have it with you. Our "Kingdom Business" is no less professional than the world's corporate pursuits. Be excellent and type your most important resource notes.

REFOCUSING

60

Refocusing is the term I use when it is time to re-center on the important. Life's demands push and pull us daily, and it is all too easy to let our devotion time suffer as we strive for productivity and squeezing yet another item on our task list into our already busy day. Stop and ask yourself, "What's the most important thing I should be doing right now?" Avoid time-wasting rabbit trails! Postpone the counterfeit urgent and keep working on the genuinely important. (1 John 2:15-17)

61

Pressing In to God is a way to resist the enemy's distractions. Use the enemy's resistance as your spiritual workout to build your faith muscles. Do not get pushed around! Get stronger in the Lord and in the power of His might! Separating yourself for a period of time to seek and hear from God may be the perfect prescription for your breakthrough. Praising God, confessing His Word, laughing at adversity, praying in the Spirit, and verbally resisting the devil are all ways to rise above adversity and maintain spiritual mindedness. (Psalm 63:8)

62

Feed Your Spiritual Hunger. Have you ever stood in front of a refrigerator not knowing what you were hungry for? I have felt that same way spiritually at my morning devotional time. Expect that your connection with God will be awesome every day! Just like viewing a restaurant menu, pause before starting your devotional time, and let your spirit search out what it is hungry for. Breaking the standard routine can be refreshing and enlightening. It could remind you that variety is the spice of life! (Psalm 63:1-7)

ABIDING

63 **Abiding** in Christ is having a continual awareness of His presence, acknowledging Him, and seeking to live according to His Word. All we think, say and do affects our relationship with Him. He is always with us in the person of the Holy Spirit. Jesus is the vine; we are the branches. Our fruitfulness depends wholly on how we treasure and pursue this abiding relationship with God. Seeking God is our #1 priority, which causes all of life to shift into proper place. (John 15:4-8)

64 **Attending Church Services** with other believers is necessary, even with the advent of media devices that bring the services to us. Technology is not a substitute for fellowshipping with believers, worshiping God and sitting under an anointed pastor who hears from God. The local church carries hope for a lost and dying world. Choose to be a vital part of a community of believers; give of your time and talents to build God's kingdom and win the lost! (Hebrews 10:25)

65

Attending Christian Events, Meetings, and Fellowships. The more we immerse ourselves with matters of the kingdom of God, the stronger our connection with our spiritual Source. Praying together at prayer services and attending church-sponsored events will keep us in a community of believers who, like us, are God chasers and on fire for Him! Let Christ form a new culture in your life of faith and love that you can bring to your world. (Zechariah 8:20-23)

66

Working and Serving in the local church gives believers a sense of ownership and belonging. We get to know other members and are able to exercise our gifts and passions to build up the Body and minister to the needs of others. We learn to love people in practical ways, showing kindness and building a sense of community with like-minded believers. Let serving others become an everyday lifestyle, in every environment. (Galatians 5:13)

67

Working on Your Assignment. A wonderful by-product of spending time with God is that He begins to give clarity on identifying your calling and assignment. Commit to sharpen your skills and perfect your gifts. As you give yourself to that calling and work on your assignment, it gives a greater sense of purpose and personal fulfillment. God's Word says, "Write the vision." Dream big and imagine where God will take you! (Habakkuk 2:2-3)

68

Stepping Out in Faith. It's impossible to spend this much time with God and not be inspired to step out beyond your comfort zone and make a difference in this world! Has God placed someone in need of a good deed on your heart? Doing acts of kindness creates a real connection with the unseen and living God. You are blessed as much as those you are a blessing to! (Romans 1:16-17, James 2:26)

PRESSING IN

69

Keeping Your Devotion Time Exciting is easy when we add variation to our activities. The Creator of the universe has much to teach us, so let us resist doing all the talking! Stay hungry for God and be open to changes in your daily devotional time. Avoid the rut of routine and do not let monotony turn you into a spiritual couch potato! Converse with God throughout the day, ask for His wisdom and guidance, and expect it! (Ephesians 6:18)

70

Pressing Through Dry Times. Ever feel like Jeremiah, the weeping prophet, whose prayers for Israel seemed to have been to no avail? Or David, when he felt God had abandoned him? All of us experience times when that connection between heaven and earth is woefully silent! Fret not. God rewards the life of a living sacrifice. Press in, stay faithful, ask for wisdom, repent if necessary, stay in faith, resist the devil and receive your breakthrough! (Jeremiah 17:5-8)

71

To Plan or Not to Plan?
Is it better to plan our devotions or simply spontaneously see where the Spirit leads us each day? Try it both ways and see that good results come with either choice! Having a plan can help you manage your time effectively, but more than once I have found myself ignoring the clock and the plan when the revelation starts flowing! And remember, God will bless your day even when distractions (and oversleeping the alarm) disrupt your best-made plans. (Proverbs 16:9)

72

It's Time For Miracles! It is in times of great opposition that God's miracle-working power brought great deliverance; usually by the faith, confession and obedience of one who believed God. Taking time to get to know God qualifies you for the exploits promised to those who follow Him. It is according to your faith. Defy adverse circumstances with a bold declaration of faith! Be willing to look foolish acting under the authority of the anointing. (Daniel 11:32, John 14:12, Mark 16:15-20, Matthew 9:29)

73

Finding Your "Flow" is time well spent. As you commit to spending time with God on a regular basis, it may feel forced or mechanical, but keep it up. The Lord is a good confidant and friend. In no time, you will be eagerly anticipating your time in the secret place. Rigid duty will give way to righteous delight! Your days will fall into a rhythm, and you will find that time with God will cover you in His presence all day long. (Psalm 119:97)

74

"Prayer Props" can keep your devotional times fun and creative. Post photos on a prayer poster of people to pray for. Create a visual bucket list. Use local, national or global maps as visual aids for prayer. Write scriptures on index cards to meditate and keep in your purse, pocket or taped around the house! Keep a notebook with sections on various prayer and faith topics. Collect knick knacks that provoke a quick prayer as you pass by them. Be inspired to lift a quick prayer to God as part of your daily walk.

75

Devotion "on the Go" is where we find ourselves occasionally when it seems there are not enough hours in the day! Thank God that as we acknowledge Him, He directs our path. The practice of speaking to God all throughout the day makes devotions with God a spontaneous, never-ending conversation. He can be reached at times other than before the rooster crows! Jesus said "I am with you always," so why not include Him as you go? (Matthew 28:20)

76

Heart-to-Heart Talks with God. These can be glorious, intimate times or heart-wrenching, tear-filled, agonizing cries to the Lord for help. We can be real with God. Talk things out with Him. Press Him for understanding and guidance when under pressure and discouraged. Draw near to Him, even on your worst day, and He will be there for you. Life is a journey. Experience it with your God! Take off the masks that hide and the pretense used to impress people. Like the skin that you are in. God accepts you, and He will perfect you. (Psalm 63)

RESISTING TEMPTATION

77

Resisting the Temptation to buckle under pressure is a discipline that works purely from obedience to acting on the Word, rather than possessing a feeling of being an overcomer. Whether the source of pressure is the enemy or people he is using to get on our last nerve, we must exercise our authority over the wicked one through speaking God's Word, saying "It is written...." This is how we enforce the victory Christ has won for us on the cross. Holding our tongue and resisting the temptation to act outside of love are also ways to stay under God's loving authority and away from the devil's territory of rebellion and selfishness. Strengthen your spirit in the Word of God so that your flesh is too weak to push you across the line. Choosing the right thing ahead of time is easier than staring temptation in the face in times of weakness. Consistently believe and speak words of faith to reprogram your mind and habits, and the flesh will submit to more godly desires. (James 1:12-13, 4:7, Matthew 26:41)

78

Habitually Walking in the Truth is the narrow way that leads to life. Choosing to do God's will is a proactive way of resisting the devil. Living for God and not self will open the way for God's involvement in our lives and shuts the door in the enemy's face. Even ignoring our adversary is a way to give him no place. The Bible tells us to either resist the devil, cast out devils or walk over them. You decide which applies! (3 John 1:3-4, John 8:31-32, Matthew 7:13-14)

79

Having Done All to Stand, Stand, because you are already an overcomer and more than a conqueror! Utilize every method in this book to dominate the enemy's tactics, hold your ground, and then advance! Breakthrough can come through any number of these activities, and when it does come, you will definitely know. The fruit of your breakthrough will flood you with peace and freedom, and the toil of living life through self-effort alone will leave. (Ephesians 6:10-13)

80

Laughter is a faith response, expressing our trust that God has worked it out and we refuse to worry and struggle over this issue. It may be a forced laugh at first, but it shows you have cast your cares upon the Lord. You can resist the devil and cause him to flee through your laughter. Laughter is like medicine. It releases those feel-good endorphins, strengthens our immune system and relieves physical and emotional pain. (Psalm 37:13, Proverbs 17:22)

81

Speaking Directly to the Enemy uses our authority over him to remove him, demons, and his influence. James 4:7 commands us to submit to God, resist the devil and he will flee from us. Luke 10:19 says Jesus gave us authority over all the devil's power and Matthew 28:18 says all power has been given to Jesus. Quote God's Word in the Name of Jesus and plead the blood of Jesus over your cause because we win! Do not let the enemy hinder your God connection!

82

Speaking to Mountains in Mark 11:23 is a metaphorical way to teach us the power of our words. Like God, we create with our words; which means we can also fix, restore, replace, increase, repurpose, redefine and re-script with our words. Instead of saying what is, create what should be. Our words are spirit and more powerful than the biggest, most impossible natural reality. Doubt not. Believe those things you say will come to pass and you will have whatsoever you say!

83

Being Strong in the Lord and in the power of His might (Ephesians 6:10) is choosing to express our faith from a place of strength instead of yielding to the pressure against our flesh and our minds. The enemy presents us with images and feelings of fear, failure, hurt, abandonment, sorrow, poverty, anger, revenge, hatred, sorrow, laziness, hopelessness, and the list goes on. Do not fall for it. Get full of God's Word and let it work for you! Use God's strength and might by faith!

RECOVERING

84

On Those "Crazy Days" where things seem to be going haywire, speak your faith and keep the praises flowing. Do not let events rule your profession; use your words to cause your life to line up with God's promises. Feelings fade. Trouble must give way to comfort. Cry out to God (Psalm 71) and declare His truth. "Let us hold fast the profession of *our* faith without wavering; (for he is faithful that promised)" (Hebrews 10:23).

85

If A Crisis Hits, let God be your stability, your solid rock and firm foundation. The storms of life cannot wipe you out if you steadfastly commit to being a doer of the Word and not just a hearer. (Matthew 7:24-27)

Our relationship with God makes prayer and other spiritual endeavors meaningful, fulfilling and valuable. If our connection with God has been broken or interrupted through hurtful experiences, trauma, or loss, despondency can threaten to widen the breach between us and God. Devotional activities can become a mundane chore and performed out of duty, void of love for God and passion for fulfilling our assignment. Our union with God is to be valued, protected and preserved. The life of God pours forth as a waterfall when our heart is whole and in sync with God's heart.

When we hurt and are wounded, the fountain of life that flows from God to us shuts off or pours as a trickle at best. Our internal mental and emotional systems begin to shut down, and we become ineffective at just about everything. We were created

to be in a constant loving relationship with God. When our behavior
and thinking is pulled downward
and away from Him, whatever the
cause, we flounder. If not addressed
we potentially become a fountain of
bitterness and murmuring and complaining "defiling many" (Hebrews
12:15) instead of "watering others"
(Proverbs 11:25).

For most believers, this regression
is subtle and entirely unintentional!
Without the strength and assurance
we need from our Source, we succumb
to natural means of dealing with our

negative realities, which fall far short and truly miss the mark.

We esteem King David of the Bible highly for his military victories and leadership over Israel, but his psalms reveal a heart in constant conflict resisting the harsh realities of life.

What was David's secret? Psalm 147:3 says, "He heals the broken in heart and binds up their wounds."

Bring it all to God. Psalm 119 shares many ways that God's Word brings comfort (verses 50, 52, 81, 92, 95, 143, 157, 161). Call a trusted friend who you know will have encouraging words for you. Call a ministry prayer line.

Make a change in your environment for a while away from stressful elements. Learn to rest in God, for real. (Matthew 11:28-30)

86

Fight the Good Fight of Faith and never become passive, tolerant or numb to the enemy's attacks. If life has lost its vitality, excitement, and meaning, you are under attack! Oppression, depression, fear, anxiety, frustration and giving in to fleshly temptations are all a sign of the devil gaining ground, so stop him! Yes, the flesh never feels like resisting, but every attack pushes us further away from our union with and power through God. Satan is a liar, and believing his lies always brings bondage, even when disguised as a fun indulgence.

We trust you will enjoy many times spent in the secret place. We were created for love and fellowship with the Father, and that unique relationship eclipses every other thing in the earth that we could ever desire. Knowing God **is** eternal life is the best state of existence possible for man living upon the earth. God is seeking for you, no matter how deep you fall or how far you run. Do you hear Him calling? Do you sense Him there present with you, even at your worst mess-up? God favors showing mercy more than judgment, so even if the enemy or that old nature won over this time, get up and run your race, keep your eyes on Jesus and keep believing God's Word! There is nothing that can separate us from God's love. Ever. He always loves us, forever and ever! Do you believe that? Well by faith, walk in it! (Romans 8:31-39, 1 Timothy 6:12)

87

Restoring our Relationship with God. Hurts, unmet expectations and heartbreaking disappointments shut down open communication, a root cause for misunderstanding. Know that God's love for us, for YOU, is forever. He knows us. He will never leave us or forsake us. Always run to Him, even when you feel you have let Him down or fallen short. It's ok, He's seen it before, and forgave you before it happened. (Psalm 139, 1 John 1:9)

GROUP
DEVOTIONALS

88

Group Bible Studies are a good way to get a family, a team, a department or any group "on the same page," using their faith and prayers in one accord, going in the same direction. It creates an atmosphere of humility, as God is welcomed to speak to our hearts. Spiritual truths shared become a foundation for unifying hearts and minds and building relationship. (Acts 2:42-47)

89

Couple Devotions. There is no set rule on how often married couples should pray and study the Bible together, or just share what God has placed on their hearts. As they do seek God as one, this reflects their commitment to submit their relationship to God's authority. Keep God in the middle of the relationship, knowing that what you say to the one, you say to Him, for He dwells in them. (1 Peter 3:7)

90

Family Devotions are a great way to model for your children how to spend time with God. When they see parents humbling themselves to seek the Lord in prayer and for godly wisdom, they will, in turn, develop the same lifestyle. Each one can take turns contributing and praying. In time, let the children lead the devotion. Let them witness your love for God and see how much you depend on God in various settings. (Genesis 18:17-19)

91

Staff Devotions are a good way to unify the hearts of your staff around the truths of God's Word made real through godly values being lived in the workplace. Show them how ancient scriptures are eternally relevant. Goals can be realized and solutions formed as they apply your teachings and principles taught. Bring the "God factor" into the office. He makes the impossible possible. His principles apply everywhere! (Luke 11:1)

92

Small Group Prayer Meetings are an ideal way to mentor intercessors and church members who desire to know God more intimately through scripture inspired prayer. Take turns praying. This is how our current prayer leaders were developed in the early days of our church, and it lays a strong foundation for establishing a relationship with God. Members will become more comfortable praying in public. (Acts 4:23-31)

93

All Church Prayer Meetings. Prayer leaders can lead the congregation, you can break down into smaller groups for a while, you can pray from a list displayed on a screen, you can add praise and worship songs; you can include testimonies and at the end of the meeting pray for each other. God's house is called a "house of prayer" for all people, and God delights in our prayers. When the world is in turmoil, God looks for intercessors. (Isaiah 56:7, 59:16)

94

Invocations by the speaker, given at the beginning of official public gatherings and events. The tone of prayer is usually more formal, using vocabulary familiar to the public and not as intense and religious as some private prayer meetings can get! By praying, we honor and respect those present. We are God's ambassadors, asking for His watchful presence. (2 Chronicles 6:20-7:3)

95

Internet-Based Devotional Meetings. Technology now makes it possible to be present at meetings around the world in the comfort of our own home! Preaching and prayer services abound on the web. You may want to participate as if you were there, or just tune in as you go about your daily work. How blessed we are to be able to worship with congregations worldwide!

PRACTICAL TIPS

96

Tools for Inspiration abound! Use reference books, both paper and digital, concordances, lexicons, timelines, genealogy and geographical charts, study aids and outlines, maps and globes, study courses, archeological photos, Hebrew and Greek dictionaries, vision boards, assorted colored markers and pens, and you're on your way!

97

Creating the Physical Environment that is inviting and inspiring will cause you to eagerly steal away to be with God. If kneeling puts you to sleep, a comfortable couch or sitting up in bed or at a desk may suffice. For variety, a backyard patio, park, balcony or beach will do. And as a last resort, praying in a closet or even a bathroom will suffice (yes, I have prayed in both), any place to be alone can become your meeting place!

98 **Soothing the Senses** (with aromatherapy, soft music, nature's beauty, a comfy chair or sofa) can reconnect us with what's beautiful and harmonious in the world. Constant discord and disconnect between head and heart is softened by the reassurance of what calms the soul and stills the body. God is experienced as we appreciate the goodness of His creation around us. Nature seems to provoke a sense of tranquility for me. Try it some time.

99

A Portable "Secret Place" Keeping your devotional materials together in one place makes it easier to steal away a few minutes for "mini-inspiration" breaks. A portable carryall bag or briefcase with devotional materials makes it easy to change locations at home or away. If you do not have a permanent location for your Bible study and prayer, keeping everything in a portable case helps you bring your secret place to any room available!

100

When All Else Fails. When the only signal from on high is filled with static or silence, or a fog of confusion, it is time to re-fill your spiritual fuel tank! Contact a church or ministry, a prayer line or trusted friend to come alongside you until you can get your bearings. God created us to be nourished by community and connection with each other. Plug into their divine connection for a power boost! Let godly counsel from the Word inject life. (2 Corinthians 7:3, 2 Corinthians 1:3-7)

CLOSING COMMENTS

Once our connection with God is solid, there is a big world out there in darkness waiting to be plugged into God! How can we keep Him to ourselves? As long as we stay connected, His power and wisdom will be there as we share the Good News of our Savior to those who do not yet know Him. One of the greatest reasons for connecting with God is to be a conduit to connect with our Christian family for friendship and serving, and then to help the unchurched connect to Christ.

Every heart hunger being fulfilled in so many diverse ways is pointing to a need that Jesus will eagerly fill. Remember, when the light goes on, darkness automatically flees. So plug in, connect, and let your light shine! And don't forget to connect to a local church with other believers who will love you and nurture you as you mature in your relationship with God and His family on earth.

"But thou, when thou prayest, enter into thy closet, and when thou hast shut thy door, pray to thy Father which is in secret; and thy Father which seeth in secret shall reward thee openly."

Matthew 6:6

If you have never felt connected to God, if He is distant to you, **pray this prayer aloud to Him:**

"God, I don't want to live without you in my life any longer. Forgive me of my sins. I turn away from sin and give my life to you. Lord Jesus, I believe you are the Son of God, you died for my sins and rose from the dead. Come into my heart. Live your life in me and through me. Fill me with the Holy Spirit, and teach me how to love you and follow you forever. Amen!"

Now get connected to other believers through a local church you can attend to grow your faith in Christ and learn about the benefits of living the Christian Spirit-filled life, and learn how to share your faith with others!

I love you and pray for you often. Stay connected to God, and keep the power flowing!

Index

100 Simple Ways to

Connect with God

Speaking

Reading

INDEX

Reflecting

Organizing

Refocusing

Abiding

Pressing In

Dr. Veronica Winston

Veronica Brown Winston has a love for God's Word and a desire for the Body of Christ to rise to their greatest potential through practical application of God's Word in their everyday lives. She is married to Dr. Bill Winston, pastor of Living Word Christian Center (LWCC) in Forest Park, Illinois. They have three children and eight grandchildren.

As First Lady, teacher and author, Veronica is a godly role model for thousands of women.

We Would Love to Hear From You!

Hello Friends!

If this book has helped you connect better with God, please write to me. I would love to read your testimony and share it to inspire others. You can contact me at:

- vwinston@livingwd.org
- on Twitter @VeronicaWinston

OTHER BOOKS BY
DR. VERONICA WINSTON

A Simple Way To Read Through Your Bible
Divine Health
Health and Nutrition
Prayer Confessions To Dominate In The New Millennium
World Prayer Guide

To order these books, please visit www.billwinston.org or call 1-800-711-9327.